Fun and Simple State Crafts

Fun and *Simple*

Pacific West State Crafts

California, Oregon, Washington, Alaska, and Hawaii

June Ponte

Enslow Elementary
an imprint of

Enslow Publishers, Inc.
40 Industrial Road
Box 398
Berkeley Heights, NJ 07922
USA
http://www.enslow.com

This book meets the National Council for the Social Studies standards.

Enslow Elementary, an imprint of Enslow Publishers, Inc.

Enslow Elementary® is a registered trademark of Enslow Publishers, Inc.

Library of Congress Cataloging-in-Publication Data

Ponte, June.
    Fun and simple Pacific West state crafts : California, Oregon, Washington, Alaska,
       and Hawaii / June Ponte.
           p. cm. — (Fun and simple state crafts)
    Includes bibliographical references and index.
    Summary: "Provides facts and craft ideas for each of the states that make up the Pacific West
      region of the United States"—Provided by publisher.
    ISBN-13: 978-0-7660-2987-3
    ISBN-10: 0-7660-2987-5
    1. Handicraft—Pacific States—Juvenile literature. 2. Handicraft—Alaska—Juvenile literature.
      3. Handicraft—Hawaii—Juvenile literature. I. Title.
    TT23.P65 2010
    745.5—dc22

                                  2008017436

Printed in the United States of America

10 9 8 7 6 5 4 3 2 1

♻ Enslow Publishers, Inc., is committed to printing our books on recycled paper. The paper in every book contains 10% to 30% post-consumer waste (PCW). The cover board on the outside of each book contains 100% PCW. Our goal is to do our part to help young people and the environment too!

Illustration Credits: Crafts prepared by June Ponte; Photography by Nicole diMella/Enslow Publishers, Inc.; © 1999 Artville, LLC., pp. 6–7; © 2007 Jupiterimages, pp. 9 (flower), 17 (both), 23 (flower), 31 (bird), 39 (both); © 2001 Robesus, Inc., all state flags; Shutterstock, pp. 9 (tree), 23 (insect), 31 (gem).

Cover Illustration: Crafts prepared by June Ponte; Photography by Nicole diMella/Enslow Publishers, Inc.; © 1999 Artville, LLC., map; © Jupiterimages, state buttons.

CONTENTS

WELCOME TO THE PACIFIC WEST STATES!

California, Oregon, Washington, Alaska, and Hawaii are the five states in the Pacific West region. This area is referred to as the Pacific West region because it is defined by the states bordering the Pacific Ocean. Alaska and Hawaii are the newest states in the United States. These are the only states not contiguous, or connected to, the rest of the states. The Cascade mountain range stretches across three of the states—Washington, Oregon, and northern California.

California has coastal ranges near the shore. The Klamath Mountains are in the northwestern corner of the state. The Sierra Nevada mountain range is in the east, and is about 430 miles long. In southern California, the shoreline has many large, sandy beaches. The giant redwood forests are in the northern part of the state.

Oregon is known for having one of the world's deepest lakes, Crater Lake, which is 1,949 feet deep. Mount Hood, at 11,239 feet high, is the highest point in Oregon. Many state forests are part of this mountain range.

The state of Washington is known for its beautiful forests and mountains. Mount St. Helens, a volcano in the Cascade mountain range, erupted in 1980. Seattle, the largest city in the Pacific Northwest, is located on Puget Sound. A sound is an inlet, a bay, or a stream leading inland that is located on a coastline.

Alaska is the largest state in the United States. It has many high mountains and over eighty volcanoes. One of the longest rivers that people can navigate is the Yukon River in Alaska. Most of the state is surrounded by water.

Hawaii is in the Pacific Ocean. It is the only island state and is the world's longest island chain. There are 132 islands that make up the state of Hawaii, but most people live on seven of the eight main islands. On the Big Island of Hawaii, there are two volcanoes that are still active. This island was formed by five volcanoes. Hawaii has many beaches, some with black sand created by lava. The islands have many cliffs, mountains, and waterfalls.

5

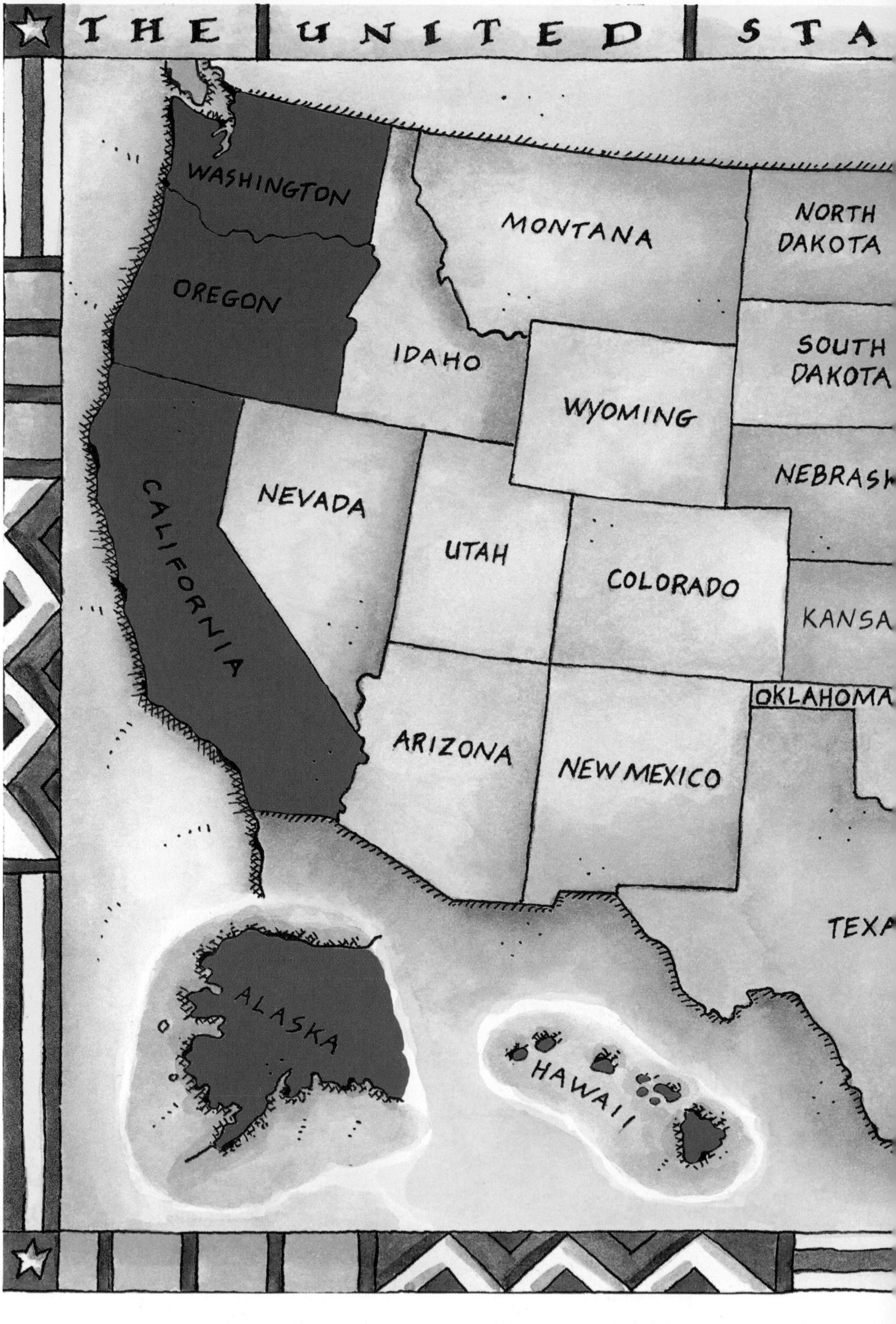
THE UNITED STA
WASHINGTON
OREGON
CALIFORNIA
NEVADA
IDAHO
MONTANA
NORTH DAKOTA
SOUTH DAKOTA
WYOMING
NEBRASK
UTAH
COLORADO
KANSA
OKLAHOMA
ARIZONA
NEW MEXICO
TEXA
ALASKA
HAWAII

Pacific West States

CALIFORNIA

Origin of name	The state was named after an imaginary island called California, in a Spanish novel written around 1510 by Garcia Ordonez de Montalvo called *Las Sergas de Esplandian.* In English, this means "The Exploits of Esplandian."
Flag	The California state flag is white, with a red stripe at the bottom of the flag. A bear in the center of the flag represents the many grizzly bears in California. A red star is in the upper left corner of the flag; the idea for the red star was taken from the Texas flag. The words "California Republic" appear below the grizzly bear.
Capital	Sacramento
Nickname	The Golden State

CALIFORNIA REPUBLIC

Motto	"Eureka!"
Size (in area)	3rd largest
Animal	California grizzly bear
Bird	California valley quail
Flower	golden poppy
Mineral	native gold
Tree	California redwood
Industry	agriculture, entertainment, aircraft, wine

MIWOK INDIAN BASKET BOWL

The Miwok Archeological Preserve was created when the ruins of a very old Miwok Indian village were discovered in Marin County, California. The Miwok Indians are known for making finely woven baskets. The Miwok Archeological Preserve sponsors classes in basket weaving and other Miwok crafts.

What you will need

* glass or ceramic cereal bowl (Ask permission first!)
* large piece of scrap paper
* tan yarn
* scissors
* masking tape
* white glue
* poster paint
* paintbrush

What you will do

1. Place a bowl on a scrap piece of paper (See A).

A)

B)

2. Tape 1 inch of yarn on the bottom of the bowl. Wet the rest of the yarn with white glue. Wind the yarn tightly around the bowl to the top (See B). Let dry.

3. Paint Miwok Indian designs (See C) on the string basket bowl. Let dry.

4. The bowl cannot be washed after the yarn and paint has dried. Use the bowl to hold knick-knacks or individually wrapped candy.

C)

MONARCH BUTTERFLY MOBILE

Pismo Beach has many thousands of visitors every winter. These visitors are monarch butterflies. Some of the butterflies fly more than one thousand miles to reach California. They come from the Rocky Mountains, and as far north as southern Canada, to escape the cold weather.

What you will need

* pencil
* poster board
* scissors
* black self-adhesive craft foam
* black permanent marker
* orange tissue paper
* black pipe cleaners
* ruler
* black elastic thread
* craft sticks
* large bead

What you will do

A)

1. Draw a butterfly onto poster board. (See page 44 for the pattern.) Cut out the butterfly shape (See A). Trace four butterflies onto black craft foam. Cut out the shapes. Carefully cut out the holes in the butterfly wings.

2. Peel the backing off the butterfly shapes and carefully place each shape onto orange tissue paper. Carefully cut around each butterfly (See B). Fold a black pipe cleaner in half, and glue to the center of the butterfly (See C). The two ends of the pipe cleaner will form the antennae of the butterfly. Let dry. Repeat for each butterfly.

B)

C)

3. Glue one craft stick on top of another to make an "x." Tie one 12-inch piece of thread to each end of one craft stick. Tie one 6-inch piece of thread to the ends of the other craft stick (See D).

4. Glue one end of each thread to the center of a butterfly. Repeat until all butterflies are glued to the threads. Let dry.

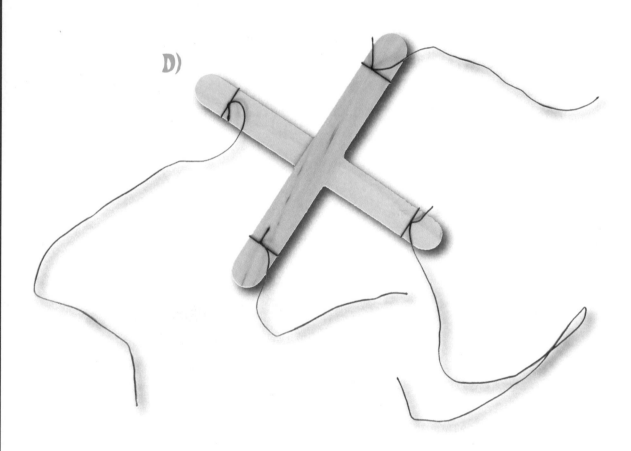

D)

5. Thread a large bead to the center of the top craft stick of the mobile and knot. Thread another piece of string through the bead as a hanging loop (See E).

E)

OREGON

Origin of name	It is not clear how the state of Oregon got its name. Historians have said it is possible that the name may come from the American Indian word *wau-re-gon*, meaning "beautiful water," but this has not been proven. It may also have come from the word *ouragan*, which means "hurricane" in French. The name Oregon was first used in print in 1778 by American explorer and writer Jonathan Carver in his book *Travels Through the Interior Parts of North America in the Years 1766, 1767, and 1768.*
Flag	The Oregon state flag is the only state flag that has a different design on both sides. It is dark blue and gold. In the center of the flag, a shield has the date 1859 beneath it, the year Oregon became part of the union. Oregon was the thirty-third state to join the union, so thirty-three stars surround the shield in the center of the flag. The shield shows the sunset on the Pacific Ocean, a Conestoga wagon, mountains, and forests. Two ships are in the background of the shield. Sitting atop the shield is the American bald eagle. Above the shield are the words, "State of Oregon" in gold letters. On the other side of the flag, in gold, is a beaver, representing the state's nickname.

Capital	Salem
Nickname	The Beaver State
Motto	*Alis volat propriis* (This is a Latin phrase which means "she flies with her own wings.")
Size (in area)	9th largest
Animal	beaver
Bird	western meadowlark
Flower	Oregon grape
Rock	Thunder-egg (geode)
Tree	Douglas fir
Industry	agriculture, timber, tourism, electronics

Oregon

VOLCANO PENCIL HOLDER

What you will need

* empty, clean soup can
* brown felt
* scissors
* self-hardening clay
* toothpick
* red and orange tissue paper or crepe paper
* white glue
* red glitter

The Newberry, South Sister, Mount Hood, and Crater Lake volcanoes are part of the Cascade mountain range in Oregon. Ground near the South Sister volcano is rising at more than an inch per year. Scientists believe this is because of underground magma. Magma is hot molten rock.

What you will do

1. Cut a piece of felt to wrap around an empty, clean soup can (See A). Glue the felt to the soup can. Let dry.

A)

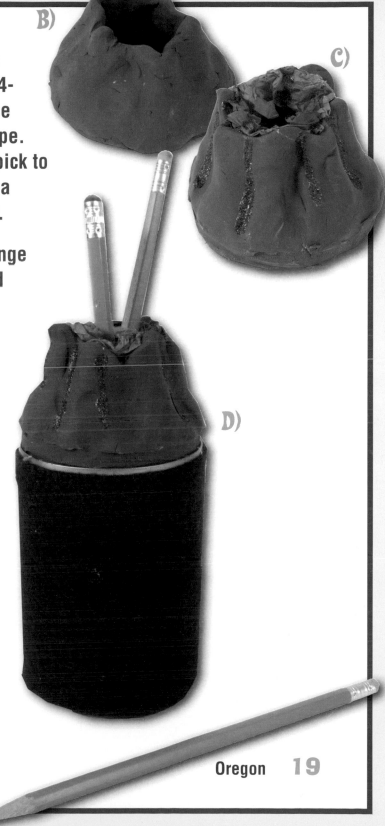

2. Flatten a 3-inch x 6-inch piece of clay to about 1/4-inch thick. Gently fold the clay to make a cone shape. Add details with a toothpick to make the cone look like a volcano (See B). Let dry.

3. Tear some pieces of orange and red tissue paper and crumple them up. Glue them around the inside top of the volcano. Glue red glitter streams of "magma" down the sides of the volcano (See C). Let dry. Place the clay cone on top of the soup can.

4. Put your pencils in the top of the volcano (See D).

B)

C)

D)

MY OWN HAT

Where can you find a hat that sings? Why, in the Hat Museum in Portland, of course! The only hat museum in the United States can be found in the Ladd-Reingold House, a historic building once owned by hatmakers. There are more than nine hundred hats in the museum. Some are antiques, and some are just very odd! The museum has a parrot hat, a fish hat, a teacup hat, and more. Hats made of beaver fur were very popular from the late 1500s to the 1800s. Many beaver trappers came to the Oregon Territory and sold the pelts to make the beaver hats. This is why Oregon is known as The Beaver State.

What you will need

* brown paper grocery bag
* clear tape
* magazine clippings of your favorite things **(Ask permission first!)**
* scissors
* white glue
* large craft feathers

What you will do

1. Fold the edges of the bag about 3 inches down. Repeat. Fold the bag along the creases on both sides. Tape along the folded sides.

2. Cut out pictures of your favorite things from magazines. Glue the pictures on the paper bag. You can glue as few or as many pictures as you like. Let dry. Glue feathers to the side of your hat. Let dry.

WASHINGTON

Origin of name	The state of Washington was named after George Washington, the first president of the United States.
Flag	The state flag of Washington is green, with the state seal in the center. In the center of the seal is an image of George Washington. On the outer yellow border of the seal are the words "The Seal of the State of Washington 1889." Washington was admitted to the union in 1889.
Capital	Olympia
Nickname	The Evergreen State

Motto	*Alki* (This is a Chinook Indian word which means "bye and bye" or "hope for the future.")
Size (in area)	18th largest
Bird	willow goldfinch
Fish	steelhead trout
Flower	coast rhododendron
Insect	green darner dragonfly
Tree	western hemlock
Industry	computer technology, aerospace industry, fishing, agriculture, aluminum smelting, forestry

TROLL PAPERWEIGHT

What you will need

* self-hardening clay
* ruler
* poster board
* pencil
* scissors
* toothpick
* plastic knife
* poster paint
* paintbrush
* white glue
* wiggle eyes

There is a troll under a bridge in Seattle, Washington! He is known as The Fremont Troll, and he is really an 18-foot-tall sculpture. He was made by Steve Badanes, a professor of architecture, and artists Donna Walter, Will Martin, and Ross Whitehead. The troll won a contest and was built for the town of Fremont's arts council. The troll has a car hubcap for an eye, and is clutching a real Volkswagen Beetle car in his hand.

What you will do

1. Flatten a 3-inch x 5-inch piece of clay until it is about 1/4-inch thick. Set aside.

2. Draw a troll onto poster board. (See page 45 for the pattern.) Cut out the poster board pattern, and place it on top of the clay. Trace around the clay with a toothpick. Cut out the troll with a plastic knife.

3. Add a clay nose and mouth to your troll. Smooth the edges of these pieces to the face of the troll. Let dry.

4. Paint the troll as you wish. Let dry. Glue on wiggle eyes. Let dry. Use the troll as a paperweight.

My Sock Puppet

The Aurora Valentinetti Puppet Museum is in Bremerton, Washington. The museum is home to nearly six hundred puppets from around the world. There are many different puppets, including animal puppets, an Alice in Wonderland puppet from the 1940s, and fancy Chinese puppets. The museum also has Indonesian shadow puppets, which are made of leather or flat wood. The shadows of these puppets are used to tell a story.

What you will need

* sock (Ask permission first!)
* white glue
* wiggle eyes or buttons
* felt and fabric scraps
* scissors
* fluffy craft feathers
* extra trim (sequins, etc.)

For children who would like to learn about puppets, the museum also holds puppet workshops.

What you will do

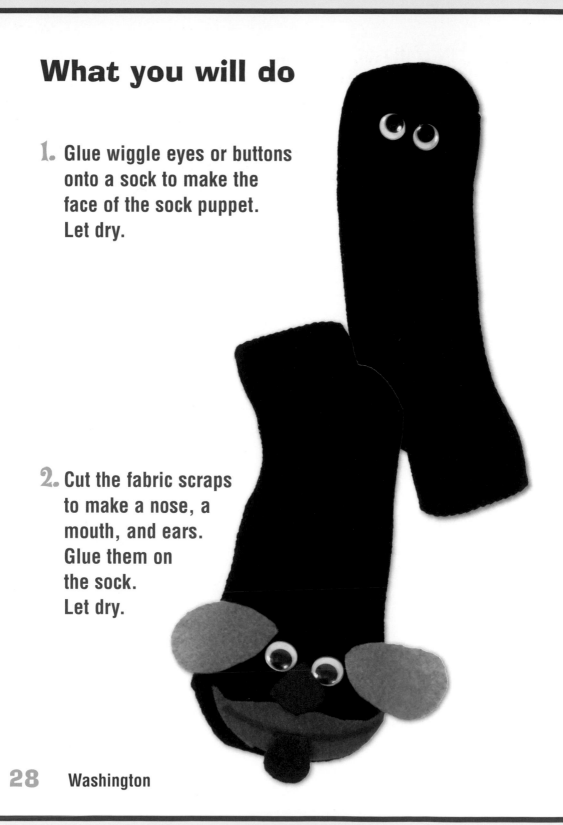

1. Glue wiggle eyes or buttons onto a sock to make the face of the sock puppet. Let dry.

2. Cut the fabric scraps to make a nose, a mouth, and ears. Glue them on the sock. Let dry.

3. Glue fluffy craft feathers to the
top of the head. Let dry. Add
details with extra trim if desired.

ALASKA

Origin of name	The state of Alaska received its name from the Aleut word *alasxaq*, which means "great land." The Aleut are one of the native tribes in Alaska.
Flag	The state flag of Alaska was created by a thirteen-year-old boy named John Ben "Benny" Benson. John was living in an orphanage in Seward when he entered a contest to design the Alaskan state flag. John made a blue flag with eight gold stars on it, representing the Big Dipper and the North Star. The North Star represents the state of Alaska. The blue background represents the sky and the state flower, the forget-me-not.

Capital	Juneau
Nickname	The Land of the Midnight Sun
Motto	"North to the Future"
Size (in area)	1st largest
Bird	Alaska willow ptarmigan
Fish	king salmon
Flower	forget-me-not
Gem	jade
Tree	Sitka spruce
Industry	salmon, oil, gold, tourism

TOTEM POLE

Totem poles were carved and painted by Tlingit, Haida, and other American Indian clans in what is now known as Alaska. The Ojibwa Indian word *totem* means the symbol for a northwest native Indian clan, or group. Totems served the purpose as a billboard or a gravestone would today. American Indians carved people and animals on their totems to share information about their clan. Think about what a totem for your family or town might look like.

What you will need

* paper towel tube
* brown felt
* scissors
* white glue
* scraps of construction paper
* pencil
* ruler
* markers
* two small craft sticks

What you will do

1. Cut the brown felt to cover and
fit the cardboard tube. Glue
the felt to the tube. Let dry.

2. Draw animals or people on construction paper for your totem.
Each animal or person should be about 3 inches tall and no
more than 2 1/2 inches wide. Cut out the pictures and glue
them on the tube. Let dry. If desired, cut out and color arms or
wings to add to your pictures. Glue them to the sides of the
tube. Let dry.

3. Color two small craft sticks with a marker. Glue to the bottom of the totem pole. Let dry.

ALASKAN FLAG

John Ben "Benny" Benson was a thirteen-year-old boy from Chignik, a small village. He entered a flag-designing contest in 1927, and his design won the

contest. The flag is blue with gold stars. It shows the Big Dipper, which is part of the constellation Ursa Major, on the left. The big star on the right represents the North Star, Polaris.

What you will need

* poster board
* permanent black marker
* scissors
* gold stiff felt
* navy blue felt
* white glue

What you will do

1. Draw a large star onto poster board with a marker. Draw a smaller star. (See page 44 for the patterns.) Cut out the stars.

2. Trace seven small stars, and one large star onto the gold felt. Cut out the stars.

3. Measure a 1-inch strip along the long edge of the gold felt. Cut out the strip and glue it to the short side of the navy blue felt.

4. Glue the small stars onto the navy blue felt to form the Big Dipper. Glue the large star in the upper right corner of the navy blue felt. Let dry.

HAWAII

Origin of name	Historians are not sure of the origin of this state's name. Perhaps it comes from the name of the Polynesian chief who discovered the island, Hawaii Loa. The islands also could have taken their name from the words *Hawa* and *ii*, which translates as a "new" or "small homeland." Hawaii is the only state that has an official native language. The name of the language spoken by the native people of Hawaii is Hawaiian.
Flag 	The Hawaiian state flag has eight red, white, and blue stripes. The stripes represent the eight main Hawaiian Islands. The British flag, the Union Jack, is in the top left corner. It shows Hawaii's relationship with Great Britain in the past. From A.D. 400 to 600, Polynesians from other Pacific islands came to live in Hawaii. Much later on, in 1778, Captain James Cook visited the islands and called them the Sandwich Islands.

Capital	Honolulu
Nickname	The Last Frontier
Motto	*Ua mau ke ea o ka aina i ka pono* (This is a Hawaiian phrase which means "the life of the land is perpetuated in righteousness.")
Size (in area)	43rd largest
Bird	nene (Hawaiian goose)
Flower	hibiscus
Gem	black coral
Marine mammal	humpback whale
Tree	kukui (candlenut)
Industry	tourism, food processing, agriculture: sugarcane, pineapples, macadamia nuts

SURFBOARD BOOKMARK

What you will need

* yellow poster board
* colored markers
* scissors
* construction paper
* white glue
* clear contact paper
* glitter pen

As far back as 2000 B.C., Polynesians were surfing in the Pacific Ocean. They called a long wooden surfboard an *olo*. The longest olos, about 18 feet to 25 feet in length, were for royalty. The olos were carved from a light wood with tools made of stone or bone. Charcoal and juice from trees was used to stain the boards. The olos were then polished with oil from nuts.

What you will do

1. Draw a surfboard shape on the poster board. (See page 45 for the pattern.) Cut it out (See A). Draw three or four small fish on construction paper. Cut out the fish. Color with markers. Glue onto the surfboard. Let dry.

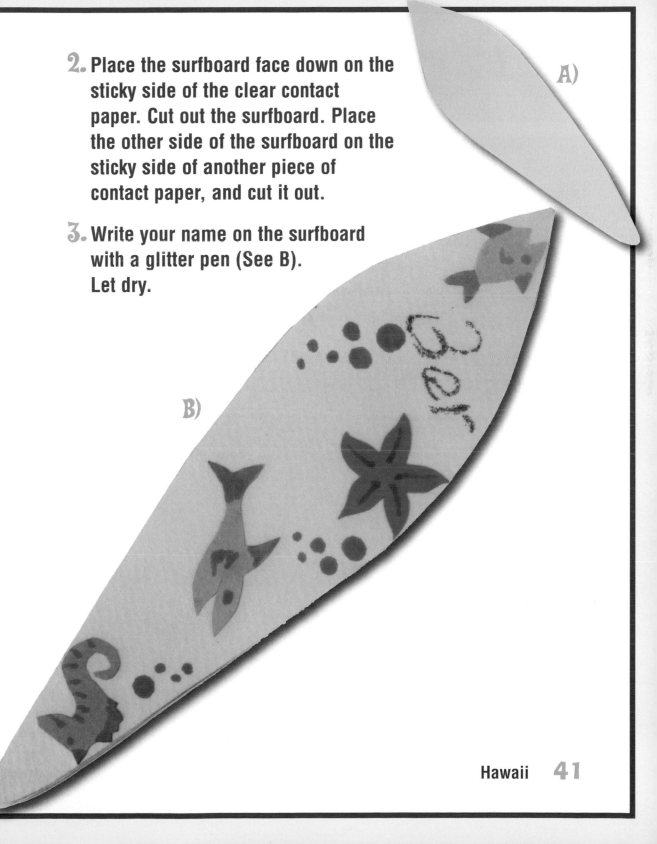

2. Place the surfboard face down on the sticky side of the clear contact paper. Cut out the surfboard. Place the other side of the surfboard on the sticky side of another piece of contact paper, and cut it out.

3. Write your name on the surfboard with a glitter pen (See B). Let dry.

A)

B)

NENE MAGNET

The nene (pronounced "nay-nay"), or Hawaiian goose, is the state bird of Hawaii. By 1951, the nene was nearly extinct because of overhunting. The nene was named the state bird in 1957. Programs were started to protect and save the nene. The bird is on the list of endangered species. Today there are about five hundred wild nene in Hawaii.

What you will need

* pencil
* white poster board
* scissors
* permanent markers
* clear contact paper
* self-adhesive magnet strip

What you will do

1. Draw a nene on poster board. (See page 46 for the pattern.) Cut it out.

2. Color in the nene with markers. Let dry. Place the nene face down on the sticky side of clear contact paper. Cut around the nene.

3. Stick a magnet onto the back of the nene. Place it on the refrigerator.

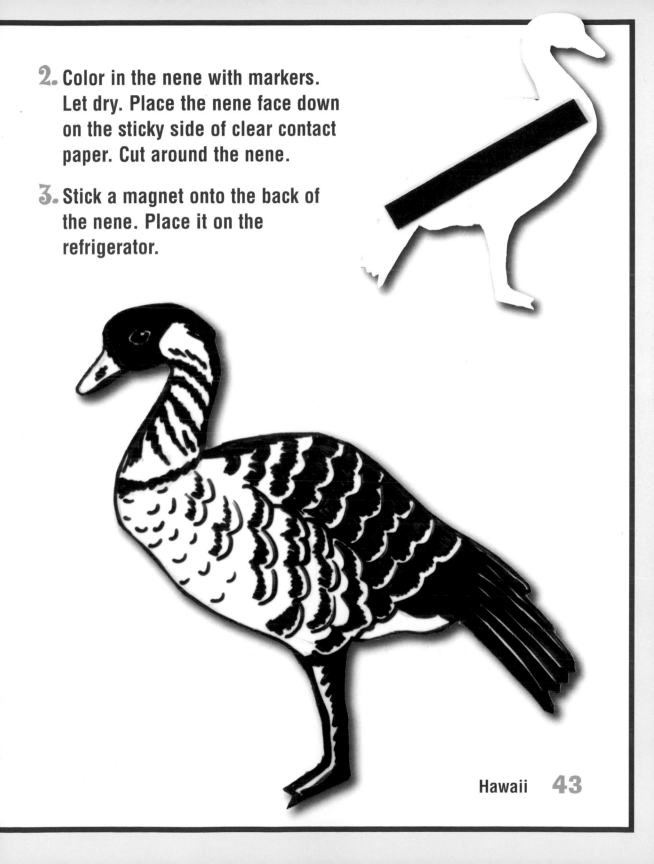

PATTERNS

Use tracing paper to copy the patterns on these pages. Ask an adult to help you cut and trace the shapes.

Alaskan Flag

At 100%

Monarch Butterfly Mobile

At 100%

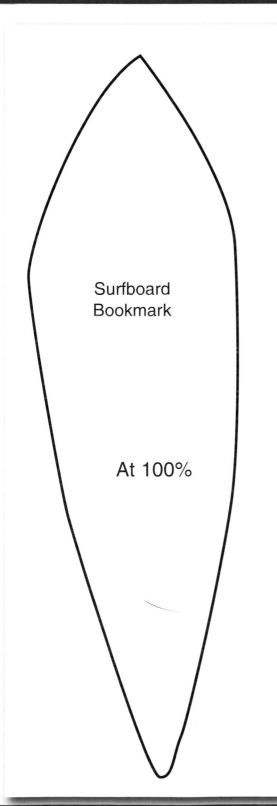

Surfboard
Bookmark

At 100%

Troll Paperweight

At 100%

45

Nene Magnet

At 100%

LEARN MORE

Books

Boekhoff, P. M. and Jonatha A. Brown. *Washington*. Milwaukee, Wisc.: Gareth Stevens Pub., 2006.

Gaines, Ann Graham. *Hawaii*. New York: Benchmark Books, 2007.

Gill, Shelly. *Alaska*. Watertown, Mass.: Charlesbridge, 2007.

Orr, Tamra B. *California*. New York: Children's Press, 2008.

Stefoff, Rebecca. *Oregon*. Tarrytown, N.Y.: Marshall Cavendish Benchmark, 2006.

Internet Addresses

50states.com
    <http://www.50states.com/>

U.S. States
    <http://www.enchantedlearning.com/usa/states/>

INDEX